"MY ROLE IN SOCIETY, OR ANY ARTIST'S OR POET'S ROLE, IS TO TRY AND EXPRESS WHAT WE ALL FEEL. NOT TO TELL PEOPLE HOW TO FEEL. NOT AS A PREACHER, NOT AS A LEADER, BUT AS A REFLECTION OF US ALL."

JOHN LENNON

1940–1980

ABDO
Publishing Company

JOHN LENNON

LEGENDARY MUSICIAN & BEATLE

BY JENNIFER JOLINE ANDERSON

CREDITS

Published by ABDO Publishing Company, 8000 West 78th Street, Edina, Minnesota 55439. Copyright © 2010 by Abdo Consulting Group, Inc. International copyrights reserved in all countries. No part of this book may be reproduced in any form without written permission from the publisher. The Essential Library™ is a trademark and logo of ABDO Publishing Company.

Printed in the United States of America,
North Mankato, Minnesota
092009
102009

♻ PRINTED ON RECYCLED PAPER

Editor: Paula Lewis
Copy Editor: Erika Wittekind
Interior Design and Production: Kazuko Collins
Cover Design: Becky Daum

Opening quotation: Andrew Solt and Sam Egan. *Imagine: John Lennon*. New York, NY: Macmillan, 1989. 242.

Library of Congress Cataloging-in-Publication Data
Anderson, Jennifer Joline.
   John Lennon : legendary musician & beatle / Jennifer Joline Anderson.
      p. cm. — (Lives cut short)
   Includes bibliographical references (p.   ).
   ISBN 978-1-60453-790-1
   1. Lennon, John, 1940-1980—Juvenile literature. 2. Rock musicians—England—Biography—Juvenile literature. I. Title.

   ML3930.L34A78 2010
   782.42166092--dc22
   [B]
                                          2009034354

Table of Contents

1

BEATLEMANIA
IN AMERICA

he Beatles, four ordinary lads from
Liverpool, England, had rocketed to
fame in Great Britain with a series
of hits including "She Loves You,"
"Please Please Me," and "Love Me Do." They had
sold more than 2.5 million records and were stars
in their homeland. Fans chased them through
the streets; girls shrieked, sobbed, and fainted.
The Beatles had successfully toured in Sweden,
France, Spain, and Italy.

But as their plane crossed the Atlantic on
February 7, 1964, bringing the group to their

▶ THE BEATLES (*LEFT TO RIGHT*): RINGO STARR, GEORGE
HARRISON, PAUL MCCARTNEY, AND JOHN LENNON

first appearance in the United States, the four young rock musicians—John Lennon, Paul McCartney, George Harrison, and Ringo Starr— were nervous. After all, they were headed to the country where rock and roll began. America had its own stars, including the Beatles' idol, Elvis Presley. Would American teens even notice the Beatles? Would the band be a complete flop? Lennon just hoped they would do all right.

The pilot radioed ahead to John F. Kennedy Airport in New York City. He called out from the cockpit, "Tell the boys there's a big crowd waiting for them."[1] Sure enough, when the Beatles stepped off their Pan Am jet, they were greeted by as many as 3,000 screaming fans. They had only just landed, and the United States was already infected by what newspapers were calling "Beatlemania."

MEET THE BEATLES

In the months before the arrival of the Beatles, America's teenagers had already fallen in love with them. "I Want to Hold Your Hand" was first released in the United States in December 1963. It had sold a quarter million copies in only three

"We knew that America would make us or break us as world stars. In fact, she made us."[2]

—Brian Epstein, manager of the Beatles

days and was now Number 1 on the charts. On radio and television, teens heard the exciting message: "The Beatles are coming!"

At the airport, the Beatles lined up for their first U.S. press conference. McCartney was a singer and the bass guitarist. With his puppy-dog eyes and endearing smile, McCartney was often called the "cute" Beatle. Standing next to him was the drummer, Starr, whose real name was Richard Starkey. Impishly adorable with a small build and a large nose, he was known as the "funny Beatle" for his relaxed good humor. Harrison was the lanky, serious-eyed backup singer and lead guitarist. Dubbed the "quiet Beatle," Harrison had a talent for one-liners.

And finally, there was singer and rhythm guitarist John Lennon. Although all the Beatles were clever, Lennon was nicknamed the "smart Beatle" for his acid wit and poetic talent. With his narrow eyes and sharp nose, he may have lacked some of McCartney's boyish charm, but Lennon had an edge and charisma. He was undeniably a rock star.

As the reporters shouted out their questions, the Beatles responded with singsong Liverpool accents and cheeky humor. "Would you please sing something?" a reporter pleaded. "No!" the

Beatles shouted in unison. "We need money first," Lennon added, as everyone laughed. "How many of you are bald, that you have to wear those wigs?" another questioner jibed, referring to their long mops of hair. "Oh yes, we're all bald—don't tell anyone!" the Beatles replied. "Are you for real?" called a voice from the group. "Come and have a feel," said Lennon.[3]

Despite the jokes, the four young men could not imagine what lay ahead of them. The Beatles were not going to disappear anytime soon.

Something Fresh

Less than three months before the Beatles arrived, the United States had experienced a tragedy. President John F. Kennedy had been assassinated on November 22, 1963. After a dark winter of grief, the nation was ready for something fresh to lift its spirits. The Beatles proved to be just that.

Although rock music was not new, the Beatles' melodious brand of rock and roll—which some reporters were now calling the "British Beat"—sounded unique. And to Americans, the Beatles' style was shockingly different. Their long hair looked girly compared to the short haircuts most American boys wore at the time. The Beatles' tight-fitting "drainpipe" slacks and high-heeled "Beatle boots" looked odd, too. But soon every teenager wanted to copy the Beatles' style. Boys started combing their hair like the Beatles and even bought Beatle wigs.

Not everyone welcomed the band. Some parents switched off their televisions when the Beatles appeared, thinking the group was a bad influence. But often, the more parents disapproved, the more teenagers worshipped the Beatles.

▲ In February 1964, Lennon waited backstage at the
Ed Sullivan Show for the Beatles' American debut.

A Landmark TV Appearance

On February 9, 1964, two days after their arrival,
the Beatles appeared live on the *Ed Sullivan Show,*
a popular variety program that aired on Sunday
nights. Ed Sullivan was known as a star maker—
the Beatles had truly arrived.

Sullivan announced the Beatles and gestured to the stage. The studio audience screamed with excitement. In homes across the nation, an estimated 74 million viewers—almost 40 percent of the U.S. population—were glued to their black-and-white television screens for what had become one of the most-watched television programs in American history.

As the Beatles played and sang "All My Loving," Americans had their first good look at the Fab Four in action. McCartney led with a clear, melodic voice, melting hearts with his flirtatious grin. As Harrison and Lennon harmonized on another microphone, their tenor voices blended with McCartney's. Harrison, on the lead guitar, picked out twanging notes, while McCartney strummed the low-end melody on his left-handed bass guitar. Lennon stood on the right, legs spread slightly apart as he handled the rhythm guitar. With an easy smile and head held high, he exuded confidence and charm. On a riser behind them, Starr kept the

Rock Guitars

Rock bands typically use three guitarists and several types of electric guitars. The lead guitarist plays the main melody of the song. The bass guitarist plays a lower range of notes that add to the beat. The rhythm guitarist strums the main chords of a song and, like the drummer, keeps the rocking rhythm going. An acoustic guitar, which does not have the electric amplification, may also be used.

steady backbeat, grinning and tossing his head to the rhythm.

For viewers who still could not tell the Beatles apart, the boys' names appeared on the screen. Under Lennon's name, a postscript warned starstruck females that he was married. This was a surprise. Lennon's marriage had been kept a secret from fans. The Beatles' manager feared Lennon's heartthrob status would suffer if girls knew he was married and had a son, but Lennon was relieved it was out in the open. More than anything, he hated to put up a false front.

Performing "She Loves You," the Beatles leaned into their microphones and sang while shaking their mop-topped heads. The audience was in a frenzy. At the end of the show, the Beatles sang their Number 1 hit single, "I Want to Hold Your Hand." Its simple lyrics suggested a fluffy pop tune, but the song had unexpected chord changes that made it wild and unpredictable. Lennon's raw, passionate voice

More Than a Fad

Critics of the Beatles complained that the band's lyrics were silly and their hairdos were a gimmick. However, it was clear that the Beatles were more than just another teenybopper fad. American singer-songwriter Bob Dylan was one who took notice: "They were doing things nobody was doing. Their chords were outrageous, just outrageous, and their harmonies made it all valid . . . . I knew they were pointing the direction where music had to go."[4]

soared with the others in rising harmony; the song conveyed a reckless longing that stirred the hearts of teenagers.

WORLD STARS

During the rest of their two-week visit, the Beatles filmed two more shows for *Ed Sullivan*. They performed for a packed house at Washington Coliseum in the nation's capital. From Washington DC, the group headed to New York City and played two shows in one night at Carnegie Hall. By the time the Beatles returned to England on February 22, 1964, teens were going crazy buying the Beatles' music. In April, the top five songs in the United States were all by the Beatles. They had achieved three consecutive Number 1 hits with "I Want to Hold Your Hand," "She Loves You," and "Can't Buy Me Love."

The band members were shocked and thrilled by their success. There was no doubt that they had conquered the United States and were true world stars.

Beatles Week

Since 1958, *Billboard* magazine has published weekly music charts listing the top-selling songs and albums in the United States. Incredibly, in the week of April 4, 1964, the top five songs on *Billboard*'s "Hot 100" chart were all by the Beatles:
1. "Can't Buy Me Love"
2. "Twist and Shout"
3. "She Loves You"
4. "I Want to Hold Your Hand"
5. "Please Please Me"

▲ IN FEBRUARY 1964, THE BEATLES PERFORMED ON THE *ED SULLIVAN SHOW.*

2

GROWING UP
IN LIVERPOOL

hroughout the fall of 1940, in the midst of World War II, Adolf Hitler ordered the bombing of Great Britain. Sirens screamed each evening, alerting citizens to take cover from the Nazi planes. It was during one of these nightly air raids, in the city of Liverpool, England, on October 9, 1940, that John Winston Lennon was born.

John's father, Alfred "Alf" Lennon, was at sea with the British navy during the war. He would not be with Julia Stanley Lennon when she gave

▶ AS A PORT CITY, LIVERPOOL WAS HEAVILY HIT DURING THE BLITZKRIEG IN WORLD WAR II.

birth to their son. But Julia's older sister, Mimi, rushed through the streets to get Julia to the hospital, finding her way through the darkened city by the light of exploding bombs.

A ROCKY START

John's mother, Julia, was a pretty, lively, auburn-haired woman who could sing, dance the jitterbug, and play the ukulele and the banjo. She was only 14 when she met Alf Lennon. Like Julia, Alf sang and played the banjo. Both were happy-go-lucky dreamers who were always up for a good time.

Although Alf was charming, he could not hold down a job. Despite her family's disapproval, Julia married him in 1938. Their only child, John, was born two years later. The family settled in a suburban district of Liverpool called Penny Lane.

John was only four when Alf ran away from the navy

The Blitz in Britain

During World War II (1939–1945), Nazi leader Adolf Hitler conquered a large area of Europe that included Poland, Austria, Belgium, the Netherlands, and much of France. In the fall of 1940, Hitler set about conquering Great Britain through a heavy bombing campaign known as the blitzkrieg, or lightning war. Liverpool, a major port through which Britain brought in weapons and supplies, became a key target of the blitz.

By May 1941, the deadly bombings had killed as many as 43,000 British civilians and left more than 1 million homes in rubble. But Hitler had not won. Led by Prime Minister Winston Churchill, England steadfastly resisted German invasion. Germany surrendered on May 7, 1945.

and was missing for six months. Assuming he had deserted her, Julia began seeing other men. When Alf reappeared in 1945, Julia was pregnant with another man's child. The baby, a girl, was given up for adoption. But Julia and Alf's marriage was soon over, although they never formally divorced. Alf prepared to leave England for distant shores.

"The worst pain is that of not being wanted, of realizing your parents do not need you in the way you need them. I was never really wanted. The only reason I am a star is because of my repression. Nothing would have driven me through all that if I was 'normal.'"[1]

—*John Lennon, speaking about his childhood*

After John's father left, Julia found a new boyfriend who had little patience for her young son. John felt unwanted and unloved. He was too young to understand that this treatment was not his fault. The feelings of abandonment would haunt him the rest of his life.

In June 1946, Alf returned to Liverpool and received permission from Julia to see his son. He asked five-year-old John to choose whether he wanted to stay with his mother or go with him to live in New Zealand. John chose to be with his father, who had been away so long at sea. But when his mother turned and walked away, John ran sobbing after her. John did not hear from his father again until he became one of the Beatles.

▲ LENNON'S BOYHOOD HOME, MENDIPS, IN LIVERPOOL

HOME AT MENDIPS

Five-year-old John was sent to live with his uncle
George and aunt Mimi Smith in south Liverpool.
They had no children of their own and were
prepared to give John a "proper" upbringing.
Julia lived nearby and came to visit, but John's
home was now with his aunt and uncle on
Menlove Avenue in a cozy, seven-room cottage
nicknamed "Mendips."

While Julia was fun loving and unreliable, Mimi was stern, strict, and organized. But when Mimi tried to punish John, he could make her laugh. Uncle George, a dairy farmer, was a jolly man who recited rhymes and taught John how to solve crossword puzzles. John spent hours reading books such as *The Wind in the Willows* and *Alice in Wonderland*. He wrote poems in the style of Lewis Carroll's "Jabberwocky" and drew the characters.

Lennon's Glasses

John Lennon's circular, wire-rimmed glasses were a trademark accessory of his in later years. But when he was young, he hated wearing glasses. Not until he saw the singer Buddy Holly, who performed in nerdy black horn-rims, did he realize glasses could be cool.

"Am I a Genius or Am I Mad?"

From a very early age, John was a rebel. The headmaster at Dovedale Road Primary School reported that he was as "sharp as a needle," but to Aunt Mimi's disappointment, he earned poor grades.[2] School bored him, and he spent class time daydreaming, drawing, or clowning around.

Classes at Quarry Bank Grammar School was no different, and he added smoking and swearing to his activities. A math teacher noted, "He's on the road to failure if he carries on this way."[3] However, John did show a talent for writing and

▲ NINE-YEAR-OLD JOHN AT HOME IN LIVERPOOL

drawing. John created his own newspaper, the
Daily Howl, filled with jokes and cartoons.

Like many adolescents, John struggled with
insecurities. He showed friends two sides of
his personality. One was silly and playful; the
other was tough and bullying. When he was not
making his classmates laugh, he was getting into

fights. He liked to be the leader and have a group around him.

At about the age of 12, John began to ask, "Am I a genius or am I mad?"[4] He decided he must be a genius—but then wondered why no one had discovered him yet. John's aunt Mimi, for one, did not seem to recognize his brilliance. While cleaning the house, she once threw away all of his poetry. John snapped, "One day I'll be famous and you're going to regret it."[5]

OUT OF THE STATIC

John was a fan of the radio. Each evening, the British Broadcasting Corporation, or BBC, provided family entertainment in the form of drama, comedy, music, and news programs. John especially enjoyed comedies with silly puns and endless one-liners. Lying in bed late one night, John turned the dial on his radio. Out of the static came something rarely heard on BBC— rock and roll.

The music was coming from a radio broadcast in the tiny European country of Luxembourg. The signal was weak, but John eagerly fiddled with the dial to listen to the songs that were topping the charts in the United States. These included the early rock-and-roll hits of Bill Haley and the Comets, Carl Perkins, Chuck Berry, and most thrilling of all, Elvis Presley. "Once I heard it and got into it, that was life, there was no other thing," John said later. "I thought of nothing else but rock and roll."[6]

John could already play the accordion and harmonica, but now there was only one instrument he wanted—a guitar. In 1957, his mother bought him a cheap model called a Gallotone Champion and taught him some simple chords. Soon he learned Fats Domino's "Ain't That a Shame" and Buddy Holly's "That'll Be the Day."

Aunt Mimi was exasperated by John's playing. She hoped he would soon grow tired of it and focus on his

Teddy Boys

Although John grew up in a comfortable suburban home, Liverpool was poor. Like other major cities in Britain, it had been bombed into rubble during the war and still had not recovered. Jobs were scarce; basic supplies such as butter and gasoline were rationed in small quantities. Hoodlums called "Teddy Boys" hung out near the docks, sometimes wielding hatchets, belts, and bicycle chains. John developed a tough exterior to earn their respect.

The Teddy Boys, or Teds, dressed in a showy style. They wore tailor-made waistcoats and narrow "Slim Jim" ties; long, dark jackets with velvet-trimmed collars; and high-waisted, tight-legged trousers like those the Beatles would later sport onstage. Their hair was greased up high off the forehead. In the back, it was combed to look like a duck's tail. Some Teds formed street gangs, imitating the ones they had seen in American movies, such as *The Wild One* with Marlon Brando.

▲ AS A BOY, JOHN WAS A FAN OF ELVIS PRESLEY.

schoolwork. "The guitar's all right for a hobby," she said, "but you'll never make a living out of it."[7] How wrong she was. John Lennon had found his true calling.

3

FROM QUARRY MEN TO THE BEATLES

*I*t was a hot Saturday afternoon on July 6, 1957, and 16-year-old John Lennon was on stage performing at the Woolton village fair. He was singing popular songs such as "Come Go With Me" and "Be-Bop-a-Lula," but he made up the words as he went along. The crowd giggled when he added funny lines.

Around him were the Quarry Men, a band that Lennon had put together with pals from his high school, Quarry Bank. The other band members played the banjo, drums, and a tea-

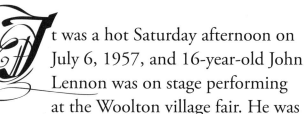

▶ IN 1957, AT THE AGE OF 16, LENNON PERFORMED WITH HIS FIRST BAND, THE QUARRY MEN.

chest bass made from a wooden crate, a broom handle, and a couple of strings. Lennon banged away on his guitar. He only knew a few chords, but it was enough to make him look like a star to the teenage fans around the stage.

This was the Quarry Men's first big performance. Lennon looked for his mother and Aunt Mimi, hoping they would be in the audience watching. Meanwhile, one person in the crowd was watching very closely—Paul McCartney.

McCartney and Harrison

McCartney had grown up near Lennon, but they had never spoken. At 15, McCartney was still a chubby-cheeked kid, while Lennon was nearly 17 and a hard-edged Teddy Boy with sideburns. "I wouldn't look at him too hard in case he hit me," McCartney later recalled.[1]

On this particular day, McCartney was with a friend who knew Lennon. When the band was done playing, the boys met up. McCartney, who was left-handed, casually picked up a guitar and played it upside down. He played it with an expertise that put him out of their league. McCartney also could really sing. He belted out Eddie Cochran's rock-and-roll tune "Twenty Flight Rock."

Later that evening, Lennon brooded. He wanted McCartney in his band, but he was nervous about sharing the limelight with someone who was as good as him—and perhaps better. "I'd been kingpin up to then," Lennon remembered thinking. "Now, I thought, 'If I take him on, what will happen?' . . . But he was good, so he was worth having."[2]

Soon after their fateful meeting, McCartney joined the Quarry Men. Later, he introduced another boy who could play the guitar—George Harrison. A wizard at learning guitar chords, Harrison impressed Lennon with his rendition of "Raunchy." Though Harrison was only 14, Lennon let him into the group. Eventually, the other members of the Quarry Men were left behind.

ART SCHOOL BOYS

Aunt Mimi despaired over Lennon. He had lost all interest in school and had failed his tests to move from secondary school to college.

The Lennon-McCartney Team

Rock historians marvel about the meeting of Lennon and McCartney, who became one of the most successful songwriting teams in history. The two boys collaborated feverishly. They skipped school to write songs and copied the words into McCartney's notebook. The boys vowed to share equal credit for all their songs under the name "Lennon-McCartney." By the end of the school year in 1958, they had as many as 20 original Lennon-McCartney songs.

Nonetheless, Lennon was able to get into the Liverpool College of Art. He began taking classes in September 1957.

Arriving at art school with his greased-up hair and Teddy Boy snarl, Lennon looked out of place, but he soon made friends. Stuart Sutcliffe, a sensitive, quiet boy, was a gifted abstract painter and knew a lot about art. Lennon learned more from Sutcliffe than from most of his art teachers. Lennon and McCartney loved Sutcliffe's personal style. Although he had no idea how to play the guitar, they convinced Sutcliffe to buy a bass guitar and join their band.

"I LOST HER TWICE"

Several years earlier, when Lennon was 14, his uncle George had died suddenly of a liver hemorrhage. Shocked by the loss of the only father figure he had ever really known, Lennon had sought comfort from his mother. Julia lived with her boyfriend, Bobby Dykins, and their two daughters. Lennon stayed at her house when he wanted an escape from his strict aunt Mimi.

But the unthinkable happened on the night of July 15, 1958. Just weeks before Lennon started his second year of art school, Julia was struck and killed by a car. "That was another big trauma for me," Lennon explained. "I lost her twice. Once when I was moved in with my auntie. And once again at seventeen when she actually, physically died . . . . It made me very, very bitter."[3]

OPPOSITES ATTRACT

In the fall of 1958, during his second year at art school, Lennon met Cynthia Powell. From the relatively posh suburb of Hoylake, Cynthia was as different as could be from Lennon. He was loud and brash; she was shy and polite. Lennon teased her by calling her "Miss Prim." But soon, Cynthia started falling for Lennon. She sensed a softer, more vulnerable side underneath his angry exterior.

Still hurting from the loss of his mother, Lennon needed stability and found it in Cynthia. Though he had been out with plenty of girls before, this was his first serious relationship. "I couldn't stand being without her," he said.[4]

MACH SCHAU!

Throughout this time, the remaining Quarry Men—Lennon, McCartney, Harrison, and Sutcliffe—continued playing gigs as Johnny

"He was rough, ready, and not my type at all. But again an enigmatic character— you couldn't resist him. He was like a Teddy Boy; he walked around without his glasses, a guitar over his shoulder, and a look that said 'Kill.'"[5]

—Cynthia Powell Lennon, describing how Lennon looked in 1958

and the Moondogs. In February 1960, Sutcliffe and Lennon came up with the name Beatals. Although the band went through a few more name changes and eventually altered the spelling, this was the name they agreed upon.

During his three years at art school, Lennon had constantly skipped classes and did not produce the required work. After failing his exams in the spring of 1960, Lennon dropped out at the school's request. He decided to pursue his music full-time.

In the summer of 1960, the group toured as the backup band for singer Johnny Gentle. That August, they got their big break—they were hired to work at a club in Hamburg, Germany. Lacking a drummer, they hired their friend Pete Best, a strikingly handsome fellow.

The German club owner wanted the Beatles to "make a show" that would please the tough crowd. "*Mach Schau!*" he shouted to them in his heavy accent.[6] The Beatles hammed it up and quickly became a huge hit. But German authorities discovered that Harrison was underage and the group

What's in a Name?

Before they became the Beatles, they were:
- The Black Jacks
- The Quarry Men
- Johnny and the Moondogs
- The Nerk Twins
- The Beatals
- The Silver Beetles
- The Silver Beats

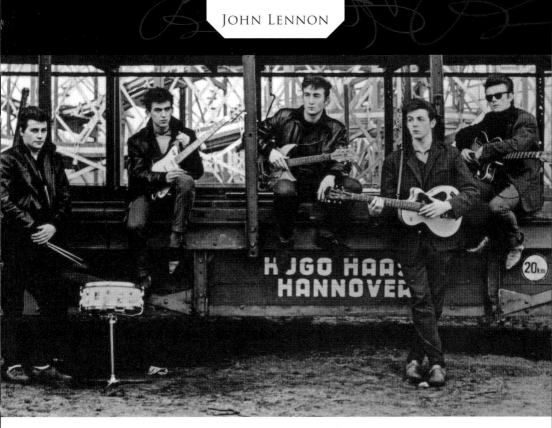

▲ IN 1960, *FROM LEFT TO RIGHT,* BEST, HARRISON, LENNON, MCCARTNEY, AND SUTCLIFFE

lacked proper work permits. The Beatles were deported to England.

THE CAVERN
When the Beatles returned home in December 1960, they were like no other band in Liverpool. Wearing black leather suits that they had bought in Germany and playing a hard, rocking sound, they stunned audiences when they took the stage. On February 21, 1961, the Beatles debuted at the Cavern Club, a dank basement club.

During the next two years, they made nearly 300 appearances.

The Beatles became the talk of Liverpool. Their pictures were featured on the front page of the *Mersey Beat* magazine. They made a record with singer Tony Sheridan called "My Bonnie." Brian Epstein, the owner of a record store, heard about the Beatles and decided to watch the group perform. When he stepped into the dimly lit Cavern Club in November 1961, he was a bit shocked. The Beatles were loud and rude. They insulted their audience and ate and smoked onstage. But the crowd loved them. Epstein was struck

Kirchherr and Sutcliffe

While in Hamburg, the Beatles became friends with a group of German art students who called themselves the "Exies," or Existentialists. Their far-out European style influenced the Beatles. During the Beatles' second stay in Hamburg, from April to July in 1961, "Exie" Astrid Kirchherr inspired the famous Beatle haircuts, which were based on her own mod French cut.

When the Beatles returned to Liverpool in 1961, Sutcliffe, in love with Astrid, remained in Germany. He planned to marry her and pursue his art career. This suited the Beatles. Sutcliffe was a brilliant artist but had never been a good bass player.

Sadly, the friends would never meet again. Sutcliffe, who had suffered from severe headaches, died of a brain hemorrhage on April 10, 1962. The news devastated Lennon.

Sutcliffe is sometimes called the "Fifth Beatle." His image appears on the cover of the Beatles' 1967 album *Sgt. Pepper's Lonely Hearts Club Band.*

by the Beatles' sense of humor and charm. He also had a feeling they would be big stars. In December 1961, Epstein asked if they needed a manager. In January 1962, the Beatles agreed to the contract with Epstein.

In order to win a recording contract, Epstein encouraged the boys to adopt a more clean-cut image by ditching the leather for suits and ties. Although Lennon hated the idea, he went along with it, hoping Epstein's instincts were right.

A RECORD CONTRACT

Epstein visited all the major record companies in London and played the Beatles' music for them. No one was interested. At Decca Records, he was told, "Groups with guitars are on the way out."[7] Finally, the Beatles got an audition at Parlophone Records with music producer George Martin. Although he liked their voices, Martin thought the songs they had written were not very good. As a band, they seemed just mediocre. But, he said, "they had tremendous charisma. I knew that that alone would sell them."[8] He signed a contract with the Beatles in June 1962.

The Beatles were ecstatic. But there was one more problem. For their first recording session, Martin wanted to use a professional drummer who had experience in the studio. Martin did not mean that Best had to be out of the band—he thought Best's heartthrob appearance was a good selling point. But his comment got the Beatles thinking.

A Change in Drummers

"We really started to think we needed the great drummer in Liverpool," McCartney said. "And the greatest drummer in our eyes was . . . Ringo Starr."[9] Starr was drummer for another band, Rory Storm and the Hurricanes. He had filled in for Best at times, and the Beatles loved how his steady beat meshed with their sound.

The Beatles asked Epstein to tell Best he was out of the band. Best was stunned and crushed. Just at the moment when the band was beginning to go places, he had been kicked out. Lennon later recalled, "We were cowards when we sacked him."[10]

Lennon, McCartney, Harrison, and Starr: the Beatles were now complete. Lennon thought they were the best band in the world. Before long, the world would agree.

A Married Man

Amid all the exciting events in Lennon's life over the summer of 1962, he had some shocking news: he was about to become a father. This was not the

▲ BRIAN EPSTEIN BECAME THE BEATLES' MANAGER AFTER
WATCHING THEM PERFORM AT THE CAVERN CLUB.

best time to become a parent. Lennon was just
22 and enjoying the rock-and-roll lifestyle, but
he would not abandon Cynthia. The couple was
married in the Mount Pleasant Registry Office on
August 23, 1962. Harrison, McCartney, Epstein,
and a few other friends attended as witnesses.

4

MAKING IT BIG

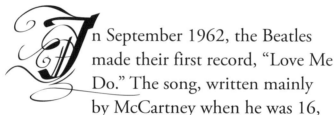

In September 1962, the Beatles made their first record, "Love Me Do." The song, written mainly by McCartney when he was 16, had a bluesy harmonica riff played by Lennon. The record sold 100,000 copies and made it to Number 17 on the British charts.

A month later, at EMI/Parlophone's studio on Abbey Road in London, producer Martin was excited. He had a song that was perfect for the Beatles, a catchy tune called "How Do You Do It," by songwriter Mitch Murray. Martin was sure

▶ LENNON BACKSTAGE AT THE TELEVISION SHOW *THANK YOUR LUCKY STARS*

this song could reach Number 1. But the Beatles did not want to become famous on someone else's song. They wanted their first Number 1 hit to be something they had written themselves.

A SONGWRITING DUO

At that time, it was not common for stars to write their own songs. Elvis Presley's big hits were penned by others; his genius was in how he performed a song and made it his own. But Lennon and McCartney wanted to write and perform.

Not technically trained musicians, Lennon and McCartney could not even read or write musical notation. But they were both naturally gifted songwriters. When they worked as a team, they could make magic. They already had a backlog of Lennon-McCartney originals waiting to be recorded.

"When we first started off writing, we used to sit down with two guitars and just strum at each other, and if an idea came out, just develop it up into a song."[1]
—*Paul McCartney, on songwriting with Lennon*

"PLEASE PLEASE ME"

For their next single, they suggested one of Lennon's songs, "Please Please Me." Lennon could remember the day he wrote it while sitting on a pink eiderdown bedspread at his aunt Mimi's.

He had been listening to the mournful song "Only the Lonely" by Roy Orbison. Mentally, he combined it with another song by Bing Crosby that included, "Please lend a little ear to my pleas."[2]

When they played the song for Martin, he found it a bit dull. Then he asked, "Can we change the tempo—make it a bit faster?"[3] The Beatles had not thought of that, but Martin was right. With a quicker tempo, the song became something fabulous. The Beatles were beginning to understand what a difference a great producer could make. With a bit more tinkering, and the addition of Lennon's harmonica, they felt they had their first megahit.

THE NEW BRITISH BEAT

"Please Please Me" was released on January 11, 1963, and was played constantly on BBC radio. The Beatles sang it on the TV show *Thank Your Lucky Stars.* Although the song stopped short of Number 1, it had an impact. People loved the Beatles' unique sound of catchy tunes with vocal harmonies, guitars, and a driving backbeat. Critics called their style "the Mersey Beat," after the Mersey River in Liverpool, or "the British Beat." This distinctive sound was Britain's answer to American rock and roll.

AN ALBUM IN ONE DAY

With the success of "Please Please Me," Martin knew it was time to record an album. On February 11, 1963, the Beatles recorded ten songs in one grueling day. By the end of the session, the band members were exhausted. Lennon's throat felt raspy, and he could barely swallow. But Martin had saved the toughest song, "Twist and Shout," for last. No one could sing it but Lennon.

Lennon gargled milk and used cough drops before stepping up to the microphone. He gave the song everything he had left. They did two takes, and his voice was gone. Lennon, always critical of his performances, thought his voice was awful—but the

Records and Albums

Before CDs and downloadable MP3s, music was released on black vinyl records. Typically, before putting out an entire album, record producers would release songs one at a time as "single" records, hoping the singles would become hits.

A single record was seven inches (18 cm) in diameter and consisted of just two songs. The featured single was on the A-side, and a secondary song was on the B-side. On the Beatles' first record, the A-side was "Love Me Do," and the B-side was "P.S. I Love You."

An LP (long-playing) record album was 10–12 inches (25–30 cm) in diameter and contained a collection of the band's songs. The Beatles' first album, *Please Please Me*, had 14 songs, seven on each side of the album. Eight of the 14 songs were new songs by the Lennon-McCartney team; the others, including "Twist and Shout," were renditions of songs that had been sung by other artists.

song was perfect. With his hoarse, ragged voice, Lennon had sounded raw, wild, and on the verge of losing control.

The Beatles' first album, *Please Please Me,* was released on March 22, 1963. By May, it became a Number 1 album and stayed there for an unbelievable 30 weeks. Fans screamed wherever the Beatles went. Beatlemania had begun!

"The last song nearly killed me. My voice wasn't the same a long time after. . . . You can hear that I'm just a frantic guy doing his best."[4]
—*John Lennon on the recording of "Twist and Shout"*

THE UNSTOPPABLE VAN

When they were not recording, the Beatles toured throughout Britain in their decidedly unluxurious van. Seemingly, the van never stopped. Lennon liked touring, but it was not always comfortable. Despite the discomfort, the group remembered this as an exciting time during which their friendships became even stronger.

The Beatles' schedule became more hectic as they toured with big names such as American star Roy Orbison. Now the tables were turning, and the Beatles were becoming bigger than their hero. Orbison asked if he could record some of the Beatles' songs.

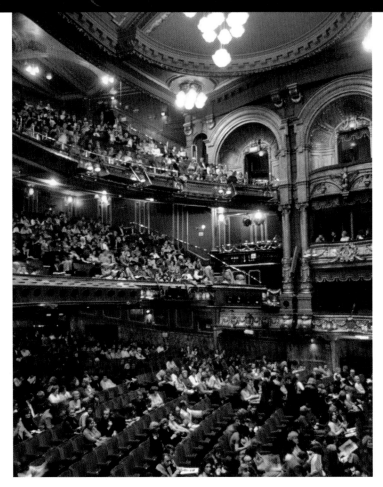

▲ ON OCTOBER 13, 1963, THE BEATLES PLAYED AT THE LONDON PALLADIUM THEATER.

DADDY

On April 8, 1963, Cynthia gave birth to John Charles Julian Lennon. Little Julian was named after John Lennon's mother. Lennon was unable to see his son for three days. In the midst of Beatlemania, the new father would have very little time to spend with his wife and child, something he would regret in later years. When the Beatles returned home to Liverpool, they were met with screaming mobs.

BEATLEMANIA!

The Beatles soon had their first Number 1 song, "From Me to You." It topped the British charts for seven weeks in May and June of 1963. It was followed by 11 more chart toppers. On October 13, the Beatles played on the popular television show *Sunday Night at the London Palladium.* Mobs of screaming, sobbing teenagers gathered outside the Palladium Theater, hoping for a glimpse of their idols. The police struggled to hold them back. Beatlemania continued to spread.

RATTLING THE QUEEN'S JEWELRY

On November 4, 1963, the Beatles were invited to play in the Royal Variety Performance hosted by Her Majesty Queen Elizabeth and the Queen Mother. The Beatles were not sure what to make

Toppermost of the Poppermost

The Beatles' success did not happen overnight. It had taken months and years to get to this point. Lennon remembered when the Beatles had stayed in miserable accommodations in Hamburg and all of the rejections they had experienced before landing their record deal. When the band members felt down and discouraged, he would ask, "Where are we going, fellas?" They would answer, "To the top, Johnny!" "Where's that, fellas?" "To the toppermost of the poppermost!" they would reply.[5]

of this invitation. They were excited about the honor, but performing before an audience of posh lords and ladies was not their kind of gig. After all, they were rock and rollers.

On the night of the show, Lennon looked out over the audience of upper-crust Londoners in diamonds and furs and let loose with some cheeky Liverpool humor. "For our last number, I'd like to ask your help," he began politely. "For the people in the cheap seats, would you please clap your hands—and the rest of you, if you'd just rattle your jewelry." Lennon ducked his head and grinned, and the band launched into a raucous rendition of "Twist and Shout."[6]

This type of remark was typical of Lennon. His message was clear. Although they had reached the top, the band would not sell out. "We were the first working class singers that stayed working class," he later said proudly. "We didn't try to change our accents."[7]

▲ EMI RECORDS HONORED THE BEATLES WITH SILVER DISCS FOR THEIR RECORD SALES, INCLUDING "PLEASE PLEASE ME" AND "TWIST AND SHOUT."

5

INTERNATIONAL FAME

he Beatles were on top of the world. They had toured parts of Europe. In February 1964, they conquered the United States. Later that summer, they made a world tour through Denmark, the Netherlands, Hong Kong, Australia, and New Zealand. Everywhere they went, Beatlemania spread. Lennon and the others could hardly take it all in. As Lennon later said, "It was like being in the eye of a hurricane. You'd wake up in a concert and think, 'Wow, how did I get here?'"[1]

▶ LENNON DURING THE MAKING OF THE MOVIE *A HARD DAY'S NIGHT*

Starr stated it well when he commented, after another exhausting day that went well into evening, "It's been a hard day's night."[2] The comment struck Lennon as hilarious. He loved what he called Starr's "Ringoisms"—flubbed expressions that came out wrong but somehow seemed exactly right. Ringoisms that became song titles included "Tomorrow Never Knows" and "Eight Days a Week."

One of Starr's expressions became a movie title—*A Hard Day's Night*. Filmed in early 1964, it depicted Beatlemania in a comic form. The movie captured the charm and wit of the Beatles. The Beatles later filmed four more feature-length movies.

THE LITERARY BEATLE

Lennon became known as the

Beatles Movies

In the days before music videos, movies were a good way to promote a band's music. The Beatles made five films:

- *A Hard Day's Night* (1964) is a comic farce in black and white and showcases the Beatles' wit.
- *Help!* (1965) is a wacky James Bond-type adventure filmed in the Bahamas, Austria, and England.
- *Magical Mystery Tour* (1967) is a surreal bus journey and contains a colorful video of "I Am the Walrus."
- *Yellow Submarine* (1968) is a comedy starring cartoon versions of Lennon, McCartney, Harrison, and Starr.
- *Let It Be* (1970) is a documentary of the making of the album *Let It Be*, which turned out to be the Beatles' last album.

"Literary Beatle" after publishing his first book, *In His Own Write,* in spring 1964. The book contains comical drawings, stories, and nonsense poems with titles such as "The Moldy Moldy Man" that show the influence of *Alice in Wonderland.*

Lennon was pleased when the book became a best seller and critics praised it as hilarious and inventive. In June 1965, he followed it with *A Spaniard in the Works.* "I like writing books," he said. "Up to now we've done everything together and this is all my own work."[3]

AMERICA AND DYLAN

All of the Beatles had been awed by the diverse music in the United States during their first visit in February 1964. Britain had only one radio station—BBC—but America had hundreds. When the Beatles returned to the United States for a concert tour in August 1964, they met a new American star, Bob Dylan. The Beatles had recently discovered his album, *The Freewheelin'*

The Beatles and Dylan

American folk-rock singer Bob Dylan was a powerful influence on the Beatles. Hearing Dylan's politically charged songs such as "Blowin' in the Wind," Lennon and McCartney were inspired to write lyrics that were about more than just girls and love. For his part, Dylan was energized by the Beatles' inventive twist on rock and roll. A popular folk singer, he would soon add electric guitars to his music, leading to ground-breaking folk-rock hits such as "Like a Rolling Stone."

Bob Dylan, and played it constantly. A young folk singer from Minnesota, Dylan was influencing the direction of music in the 1960s with his powerful songwriting. Dylan also introduced the Beatles to marijuana, an illegal drug that none of them had tried before. Soon, the Beatles started using marijuana heavily.

THE UPS AND DOWNS OF FAME

By January 1965, the constant touring and recording had exhausted Lennon. He had been drinking and smoking constantly. He felt fat and unhealthy. The Beatles felt trapped by fame. Everywhere they went, they had to stay in their hotel rooms or be mobbed by their fans.

Lennon wrote "Help!" for the Beatles' second film. He later realized the song was a cry for help. As the lyrics suggested, he did really feel "down," and he was "not so self-assured." In "Nowhere Man," Lennon expressed his feelings of emptiness. He was growing as a songwriter and now wrote more personal lyrics.

In August 1965, the Beatles made a second tour of the United States. The group that had once played in small clubs such as the Cavern in Liverpool now performed in giant stadiums. On August 15, 1965, the Beatles played at Shea Stadium in New York City to an audience of

▲ McCartney, Harrison, Lennon, and Starr posed
with MBE medals awarded to them by Queen
Elizabeth on October 26, 1965.

55,000. The roar of the crowd was deafening. It
was a historic moment, and Lennon recognized
it. "It was marvelous. It was the biggest live show
anybody's ever done, they told us. And it was
fantastic, the most exciting we've done."[4]

MEETING THE KING

The Beatles met Elvis Presley, the "King of Rock
and Roll," on August 27, 1965, at his mansion in
Bel Air, California. Presley was their idol. They

were so awed that they did not know what to say. Then Presley joked, "Well, if you're all going to just sit and stare at me, I'm going to bed."[5] That broke the ice, and they began talking and playing music together.

Lennon had mixed feelings about Presley. He loved the music Presley had recorded in the 1950s, but he felt Presley had sold out after joining the army in 1957. Now Presley was making money with films that Lennon found corny. He was not making good music anymore. To Lennon, Presley had been the voice of the 1950s—but the 1960s belonged to the Beatles.

HONORED BY THE QUEEN

On October 26, 1965, the Beatles received an honor from Queen Elizabeth at Buckingham Palace. They were being recognized as Members of the Most Excellent Order of the British Empire, or MBEs, which are part of the lowest order of knighthood. Usually, the honor was awarded to war heroes. Some people who had received the award protested that the Beatles did not deserve it. The Beatles were flattered and amused. Even Lennon could not help feeling excited and nervous

"I certainly earned a fortune as a Beatle . . . and spent a fortune. I mean, it was one big party!"[6]

—*John Lennon*

▲ LENNON AND HIS SON JULIAN POSED BY LENNON'S
PAINTED ROLLS ROYCE.

at the honor: "You can't help being impressed
when you're in the Palace, when you know you're
standing in front of the Queen."[7]

But his feelings changed. "Taking the MBE
was a sell-out for me," Lennon said later.[8] He
returned the medal to the Palace in 1969 as a
protest against the wars in Vietnam and Nigeria.

MILLIONAIRES

The Beatles were now millionaires. Instead of
traveling in an uncomfortable van, Lennon had
a luxurious chauffeur-driven Rolls Royce, which
he later had painted in bright psychedelic colors.
Lennon and Cynthia bought an estate in a posh
London suburb, although Lennon was rarely
home to enjoy it.

6

CONTROVERSY AND CHANGE

hen Beatlemania was at its height in 1964 and 1965, it seemed impossible that anyone could hate the Beatles. But in 1966, people were making bonfires with their Beatles records. It all started with a comment John Lennon had made to a London news reporter: "We're more popular than Jesus now."[1]

Lennon's comment was not meant as a boast. It was just part of a discussion he was having with the reporter. Lennon thought it was funny that teens seemed to like pop music more than

▶ ALBUMS BY THE BEATLES WERE BURNED IN PROTEST OF LENNON'S COMMENT.

religion. Typical of Lennon, he said what he thought. But the newspaper had printed his words to make them sound like an attack on religion. And now Christians in the United States, particularly in the South, were deeply offended.

At first, Lennon did not take it seriously. But as the Beatles began their U.S. concert tour in August 1966, they witnessed the repercussions of the comment. Radio stations in the South banned the Beatles and asked teens to publicly burn their "Beatles trash." The Beatles received death threats. Their manager, Epstein, urged Lennon to make a public apology. At a press conference on August 11, Lennon said:

I'm sorry I opened my mouth. I'm not anti-God, anti-Christ, or anti-religion. I wasn't knocking it or putting it down. I'm not saying that we're better or greater, or comparing us with Jesus . . . I just said what I said and it was wrong. Or it was taken wrong. And now it's all this.[2]

The Butcher Cover

The Beatles created controversy in 1966 with the cover of their album *Yesterday and Today*. The album cover showed the Beatles in white butcher's jackets, covered with pieces of raw meat and baby doll parts. The bizarre picture was the idea of an art photographer, and Lennon loved it. But when buyers complained, the picture was quickly replaced. Today, the rare butcher cover version is a valuable collector's item.

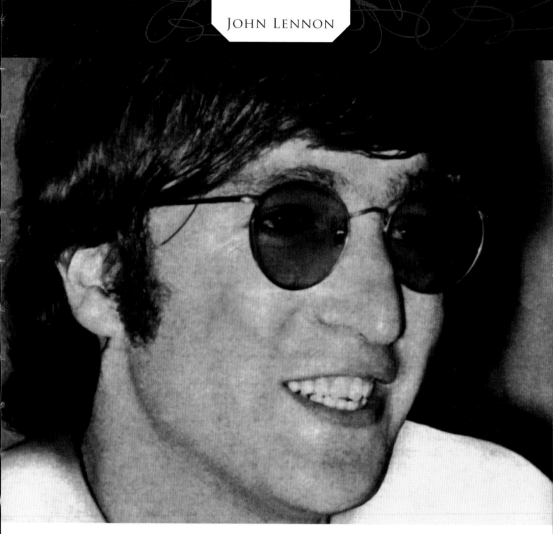

▲ LENNON IN 1966

The halfhearted apology did not help much. Death threats had the Beatles on edge. Onstage in Memphis on August 19, 1966, they heard a loud bang. For one awful moment, each looked at the other to see who had been shot. To their relief, it had only been a firecracker, but the rest of the tour was tense. Touring had become too dangerous now. And the fans at their shows screamed so loudly that no one could hear what they were singing. The Beatles decided that their concert at Candlestick Park in San Francisco on August 29 would be their last. They would never hold a formal concert again.

A CHANGING SOUND: *RUBBER SOUL* AND *REVOLVER*

When the Beatles were not touring during the mid-1960s peak of Beatlemania, they were experimenting with new sounds in the studio. One day, Lennon rested his electric guitar up against an amplifier. Feedback from the amp created a vibrating noise. They told their producer, Martin, they would use this sound. The effect was recorded for the song "I Feel Fine." For McCartney's

Automatic Double Tracking

While working on the *Revolver* album in April 1966, an engineer at the EMI studios used automatic double tracking to create layers of sound. It involved recording sound on two tape recorders at different speeds. This made one voice sound like two voices singing the same song in different pitches and speeds.

For "Tomorrow Never Knows," Lennon wrote all the music in the chord of C, which gave it a droning sound. He wanted his voice to sound like a Tibetan monk chanting from a hilltop. Studio techs used double tracking and recorded Lennon's voice through a special speaker to achieve the effect. "Tomorrow Never Knows" was the first song recorded for the album *Revolver*, but it became the final song on the album.

ballad "Yesterday," they added the gentle sound
of classical string instruments. For "Norwegian
Wood," Harrison plucked a sitar, an Indian string
instrument. The exotic instrument gave the song
a mystical quality. It was recorded on the album
Rubber Soul, which was released in December
1965. It kicked off a new sound for the late
1960s.

In spring 1966, the Beatles recorded the
album *Revolver.* That album also was packed
with interesting sounds that no one had tried on
a record before. The Beatles experimented with
recording music in reverse and used an effect
called double tracking. *Revolver* included the
song "Taxman," written by Harrison. Lennon
and McCartney had dominated before, but now
Harrison had arrived as a songwriter. "Yellow
Submarine," sung by Starr, became a Number 1
hit, as did "Eleanor Rigby." Critics raved that
Revolver was the Beatles' best album yet.

FAMILY PROBLEMS

Lennon's wife, Cynthia, had been by his side
since they met in 1958. During these eight years,
she had visited him when the Beatles played in
Hamburg, traveled with him on his first U.S.
tour in 1964, and went with him to Buckingham
Palace to meet the Queen. "No matter what's

▲ Lennon's wife, Cynthia, in the mid-1960s

happening, you know, she's always there for me,"
Lennon said about her.[3]

Cynthia was happy for Lennon's success. But
it was difficult to find time to spend together.
Lennon was exhausted when he came home from
his concerts and would sleep for several days. He
regretted not spending enough time with his son.
In a letter to Cynthia in 1965, Lennon wrote:

I really miss him as a person now . . . I think it's been a slow process my feeling like a real father! I spend hours in dressing rooms and things thinking about the times I've wasted not being with him . . . I really want him to know and love me, and miss me like I seem to be missing you both so much.[4]

Beatles Albums 1964–1966

Amazingly, while touring practically nonstop at the height of Beatlemania, the Beatles released 12 albums in a little more than two years. These included:

- *Meet the Beatles!* (1964)
- *A Hard Day's Night* (1964)
- *Beatles for Sale* (1964)
- *Help! (1965)*
- *Rubber Soul* (1965)
- *Revolver* (1966)

But instead of getting closer, Lennon and Cynthia grew more distant. Lennon had begun using LSD, a powerful hallucinogenic drug. When Lennon used the drug, he was so spaced-out that Cynthia could not communicate with him. Lennon believed he was opening his mind to new dimensions with LSD and was disappointed that his wife did not want to use the drug with him. Cynthia worried that their marriage was in trouble, and she was right.

"YES"

On November 9, 1966, Lennon was invited to an art show at Indica Gallery in London. When Lennon walked into the gallery, he thought it was a joke. An ordinary apple was placed on a stand with a price tag of £200 (approximately $4,600 today). Then he saw a ladder and climbed up it. A magnifying glass hung from the ceiling. He looked through it to see the tiny word "YES." Now he was interested. Most avant-garde art was negative, but this was a positive message.

The artist, a tiny Japanese woman with a serious face and long black hair, came up to Lennon and handed him a card with the word "BREATHE." He breathed loudly. Then he saw a sign that said, "Hammer a Nail In," and asked if he could hammer a nail in. She told him, "you can hammer a nail in for five shillings." Lennon said, "Well, I'll give you an imaginary five shillings and hammer an imaginary nail in."[5]

Yoko Ono and Lennon locked eyes. They understood each other.

———— •◆• ————

Yoko Ono and Avant-Garde Art

Avant-garde art pushes the boundaries of what is socially acceptable. It is often shocking or disgusting to viewers, causing them to think more deeply about their values and prejudices.

When Lennon met Yoko Ono, she was well known as an avant-garde artist. In 1964, she created a performance called "Cut Piece." Ono knelt on the floor, while members of the audience were invited to cut off pieces of her clothing, leaving her naked. Ono's intention was to get people thinking about how they treat—or mistreat—others in society.

▲ ONO AND LENNON IN 1968

7

THE PSYCHEDELIC YEARS

imes were changing in the late 1960s. A feeling of revolution was in the air. The civil rights movement grew violent as race riots broke out in U.S. cities. Women were becoming empowered. The war raged in Vietnam. Young people who grew their hair long and talked about love and peace were labeled as "hippies." In 1967, as many as 100,000 hippies camped out in the Haight-Ashbury neighborhood of San Francisco during what became known as the Summer of Love.

▶ People gathered at a festival during San Francisco's Summer of Love.

The Beatles were changing, too. Lennon had gone to Spain to film a movie called *How I Won the War.* He returned with his hair cut short and a pair of wire-rimmed granny specs. Harrison had gone to India to learn from legendary sitar player Ravi Shankar. He returned with new musical and spiritual ideas. McCartney had driven around France in his Aston Martin convertible, wearing a mustache and beard as a disguise. Soon all the Beatles grew mustaches. "Growing mustaches is just part of being a hippy," Starr explained. "You grow your hair, you grow a mustache."[1]

The band members no longer looked like the Beatles. They were tired of all the madness that came with their mega stardom. McCartney had an interesting idea. What if they pretended to be a different band altogether? McCartney's idea led to what has often been called the most influential rock album of all time, *Sgt. Pepper's Lonely Hearts Club Band.*

SGT. PEPPER'S BAND

The cover of this album was not an ordinary photo of the Beatles. They dressed up like a military band in fluorescent-colored uniforms, wearing their MBE medals from the queen. Behind them was a kaleidoscope of famous faces that included Edgar Allan Poe, Albert Einstein,

▲ THE ALBUM COVER OF *SGT. PEPPER'S LONELY HEARTS CLUB BAND*, WHICH WAS RELEASED IN 1967

and Marilyn Monroe. The new identity was not meant to be serious. But the music on the album was seriously good.

"A Day in the Life" is an incredibly original song. It begins with Lennon's singing, "I read the news today . . ." in a haunting voice followed by the music of a symphony orchestra. The musicians played their instruments from the lowest to the highest note, creating a frightening volcano of noise that ended with the ring of an alarm clock and McCartney singing, "Woke up, got out of bed . . . ."

On another track, Lennon's surreal lyrics in "Lucy in the Sky with Diamonds" brought listeners to a place like Alice's Wonderland with his mention of "marmalade skies." With *Sgt. Pepper's Lonely Hearts Club Band,* some fans were now convinced that the Beatles were mystic gurus, or spiritual teachers, sending messages from beyond.

"Lucy in the Sky with Diamonds"

People thought that the initials of the song stood for the hallucinogenic drug LSD, but actually, the song was inspired by a painting that Lennon's son, Julian, made of his school classmate, Lucy. Lennon explained:

My son came home with a drawing and showed me this strange-looking woman flying around. I said, "What is it?" and he said, "It's Lucy in the sky with diamonds," and I thought, that's beautiful. I immediately wrote a song about it. And . . . somebody noticed that the letters spelt out LSD. I had no idea . . . it wasn't about that at all. The images were from Alice in Wonderland. *It was Alice in the boat. . . . There was also the image of the female who would someday come save me—"a girl with kaleidoscope eyes" who would come out of the sky. It's not an acid song.[2]*

LOOKING FOR A GUIDE

The Beatles did broadcast a message all over the world in 1967. That message was "All You Need Is Love." The song was written by Lennon and performed by the Beatles on the first live global satellite broadcast on June 25. Four hundred million people in 26 countries watched the broadcast. It was an appropriate song for the Summer of Love.

"I write messages, you know. See, when you start putting out messages, people start asking you, 'What's the message?'"[4]

—*John Lennon*

But the Beatles were not spiritual gurus. In truth, they were looking for guidance. In August 1967, they attended a weeklong retreat led by the Indian spiritual leader Maharishi Mahesh Yogi. The Maharishi taught transcendental meditation, which he said allowed people to gain a higher level of consciousness. Lennon was very interested in the idea.

But while they were at the retreat, the band members received terrible news. Epstein, their manager, had died of an overdose of sleeping pills. They grieved for Epstein, who had been a great friend. They also felt a bit lost. He had been with the band since discovering them in Liverpool. He handled all their finances and business dealings—things that the Beatles could

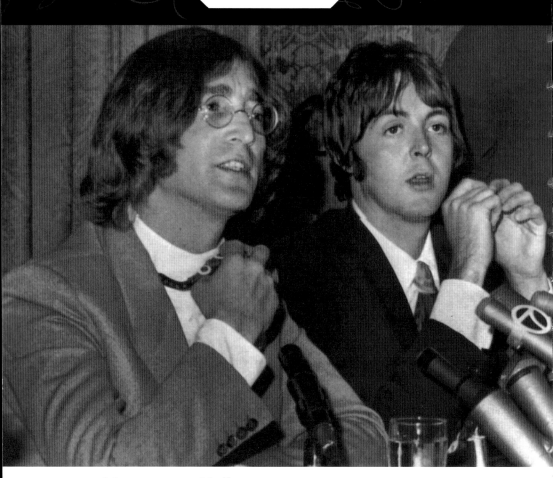

▲ LENNON AND MCCARTNEY ANNOUNCED THAT THE
BEATLES FORMED APPLE CORPS.

not do themselves. Lennon said, "I knew that we
were in trouble then . . . I was scared. After Brian
died, we collapsed."[3]

MAGICAL MYSTERY TOUR AND APPLE CORPS

McCartney now began to take on a leadership
role in the band. He came up with an idea for a

film called *Magical Mystery Tour*. In the movie, the Beatles would travel the countryside in a brightly painted bus and share bizarre adventures. Critics hated the movie, which had no real plot. But the soundtrack for the film was a success. It included "Strawberry Fields" and "Penny Lane," which were highly praised. It was also one of Lennon's favorite albums "because it was so weird."[5] The album included "I Am the Walrus," written by Lennon. The surreal lyrics only increased his legend.

The Beatles formed their own company, Apple Corps in 1968. They wanted to do everything— record their own music, publish books, and sell hippie gear in their Apple Boutique. They had a psychedelic mural painted on the company's London headquarters. However, they were forced to paint over it when neighbors complained. Apple lost money. The Beatles were not used to managing a business and creating budgets. They fought about Apple, and Lennon became annoyed with McCartney.

"Hey Jude"

McCartney felt sorry for Cynthia and, especially, for five-year-old Julian, when Lennon left his wife for Ono. He drove out to visit Cynthia. On the way, he wrote a song for Julian and called it "Hey Jules." He changed it to "Hey Jude" because it sounded better. The song became one of the most popular the Beatles ever recorded.

PULLED BY LOVE

The Beatles wanted to get away from it all. In February 1968, they traveled to India for a three-month retreat with the Maharishi. The Beatle wives, Cynthia, Maureen, and Pattie, joined them, as did McCartney's girlfriend, Jane Asher, and friends including musician Mick Jagger and actress Mia Farrow. Cynthia hoped to reconnect with her husband on the trip. But Lennon was more interested in meditation and spent eight hours a day focused on the practice. There was another reason for his distance, however. He had been receiving postcards in India from Ono.

After they returned to England, Lennon contacted Ono, and their love affair began. Cynthia, coming home from a trip to Greece some weeks later, found Lennon and Ono together in the house. It wasn't long before Lennon announced he wanted a divorce. "My marriage to Cyn was not unhappy," he explained later. "But . . . with Yoko I really knew love for the first time . . . . Being with Yoko makes me free. Being with Yoko makes me whole. I'm a half without her."[6]

▲ THE MAHARISHI MAHESH YOGI

8

LOVE, PEACE, AND AN END TO THE BEATLES

By 1968, Lennon was in love. He saw Ono as more than a romantic partner. She was his intellectual and creative equal despite their different backgrounds. Lennon had started as a working-class kid and a rough-edged rocker. Ono had been raised in a wealthy family in Japan and was a classically trained musician and concept artist. But they had something powerful in common: they not only wanted to push the boundaries of music and art, but wanted to speak out for causes in which they believed.

▶ ONO AND LENNON WITH HIS SON JULIAN IN 1968

Ono's entrance into Lennon's life created problems with the Beatles. Lennon wanted to spend every minute with Ono and work creatively with her. He brought her to the studio while the Beatles recorded their next album, *The Beatles* (known as the White Album for its stark white cover).

Soon, Ono was in the studio all the time. She voiced her opinions about the music and participated by grabbing the microphone and singing on some songs. This was unthinkable to the other Beatles. No wives or girlfriends had ever been brought into the studio before. The atmosphere became tense.

THE BEGINNING OF THE END

Lennon was ready to leave the Beatles. The White Album, which came out in November 1968, was hailed as a great success. While Lennon actually loved the music, he felt the Beatles had lost their magic. "The togetherness had gone," he said. "There was no longer any spark."[1] Harrison agreed. He was growing as a songwriter and musician and felt that the Beatles held him

"When I fell in love with Yoko, I knew, my God, this is different from anything I've ever known. This is something other. This is more than a hit record, more than gold, more than everything. It is indescribable."[2]

—*John Lennon, talking about Ono in a 1980 interview*

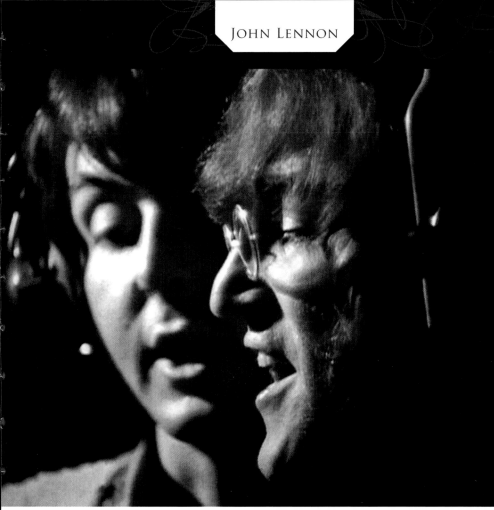

▲ McCartney and Lennon recording in the Abbey Road Studios in February 1968

back. Frustrated by all the tension, gentle-hearted Starr threatened to quit.

Determined to keep the band together, McCartney suggested that they go "back on the road, small band, go and do the clubs."³ Lennon snapped, "I wasn't going to tell you, but I'm breaking the group up. It feels good. It feels like a divorce."⁴

Harrison and Starr were shocked. At last, Lennon agreed to wait a couple of months and see what would happen. The group began working on another album and the documentary film *Let It Be*. On January 30, 1969, the Beatles shocked London by holding a live performance on the roof of their Apple Corps headquarters. The Beatles had not performed live for nearly two and one-half years. Now they were up on a rooftop, playing music in the sky! It was a wonderful moment, but it was to be the group's last performance together. It was the beginning of the end for the Beatles.

"The Ballad of John and Yoko"

The lyrics of "The Ballad of John and Yoko" tell the story of Lennon and Ono's wedding and honeymoon in March 1969. First, they tried to get married on a ferry crossing the English Channel, but could not because of an issue with Ono's passport. Next, they planned to marry in Amsterdam. However, they would have had to live in Amsterdam for two weeks to establish residency to be married there.

The Beatles' assistant, Peter Brown, suggested they marry in Gibraltar, an island south of Spain that belonged to Great Britain. Lennon and Ono flew to France to meet Alistair Taylor, an Apple executive, who brought the paperwork required for the couple to marry. On March 20, 1969, the couple was married in Gibraltar.

They later honeymooned at a hotel in Amsterdam and talked to the press from their bed as part of their Bed-In for Peace. The acorns mentioned in the lyrics of "The Ballad of John and Yoko" refer to acorns Lennon and Ono sent to world leaders to plant as a symbol of peace.

NEW UNIONS

Lennon and Ono collaborated on their own projects. Their first album, *Unfinished Music No. 1: Two Virgins,* was released a week after the Beatles' White Album. But unlike the White Album, *Two Virgins* was a flop. People did not care for the experimental music.

Even more oddly, Lennon and Ono were stark naked on the album cover. Record stores had to cover the album with brown paper. Lennon did not understand the controversy. He said, "We felt like two virgins because we were in love, just met, and trying to make something."[5] The couple followed up with two more experimental albums, but like their first album, neither of these became popular. Many Beatles fans were angry and disgusted with Lennon's involvement with Ono. They thought she was leading him in the wrong direction creatively.

GIVE PEACE A CHANCE

Lennon and Ono decided to make their partnership official by getting married. They flew to Gibraltar, an island south of Spain, and were married on March 20, 1969. Lennon and Ono knew their wedding would make the news and that the press would never leave them alone on their honeymoon. They decided to invite

▲ LENNON HOLDS THE MARRIAGE CERTIFICATE AFTER HE MARRIED ONO ON MARCH 20, 1969.

some reporters into their hotel room, where they would hold a Bed-In for Peace. As Lennon described it, this was a "commercial for peace." When the press heard that Lennon and Ono were in bed, they rushed to the hotel, hoping to see something scandalous. But they found the couple in pajamas. Lennon's hair and beard were now long and scraggly. He and Ono encouraged people to grow long hair and work for peace. "All we are saying," he told a reporter, "is give peace a chance."[6]

The Bed-In stunt was ridiculed by the press, who thought it was a ploy to promote Lennon and Ono. But peace activists paid attention. They soon asked Lennon to become an active political voice. Midway through 1969, he recorded "Give Peace a Chance." It was sung with a group of celebrities and journalists. The song became an anthem for the antiwar movement.

The Other Beatles

After the Beatles broke up, McCartney and his wife Linda had a successful career with his band Wings. He enjoyed nine Number 1 hits with Wings and other musicians. Today, McCartney is listed in *The Guinness Book of Records* as the most successful musician and composer in pop music history. He continues to perform and write music and has been knighted by Queen Elizabeth.

Starr also enjoyed success with solo singles and albums and has appeared in many films and documentaries. Today, he tours with Ringo Starr & His All-Starr Band.

Harrison pursued a successful solo career and produced hits such as, "My Sweet Lord" (from his 1970 album *All Things Must Pass*). Harrison died of cancer in 2001.

ABBEY ROAD

Later that summer, something magical was taking shape. At Abbey Road Studios, the Beatles were recording a new album. Perhaps sensing it would be their last, they worked together almost like in the old days. The *Abbey Road* album included "Come Together" by Lennon. Harrison wrote

"Something [in the Way She Moves]" and "Here Comes the Sun." Lacking an idea for the album cover, the group chose to have a picture taken of them in the street. The resulting photo of the Beatles crossing Abbey Road at a white-striped intersection became one of the most famous photos of the Beatles. Lennon, with a long, flowing beard and wearing a white suit, led the way. He was followed by Starr in a formal black suit, a barefoot McCartney, and Harrison in jeans and sneakers.

BREAKING FREE

In addition to marijuana, Lennon and Ono had started using heroin—an even more dangerous drug. After just a few months, Lennon's cheeks were hollow, his hair was a tangled mess, and his eyes held a vacant stare. At the end of summer in 1969, he and Ono went to their new home, a beautiful white mansion, Tittenhurst Park, in Ascot, England. There, John went "cold turkey"—he stopped using heroin completely. Addicted to the drug, he became very sick, but he did not give in.

The time had come, Lennon decided, to break with the Beatles. They had

"I still love those guys. The Beatles are over, but John, Paul, George, and Ringo go on."[7]

—*John Lennon in a 1980 interview*

▲ PHOTO ON THE COVER OF THE *ABBEY ROAD* ALBUM

been together for nearly ten years. Although he told the others that he was through, nothing was officially said to the press until McCartney announced it in April 1970. After 27 Number 1 hits, the Beatles, the most famous group in music history, disbanded.

———◆———

9

AMERICA,
FATHERHOOD,
AND TRAGEDY

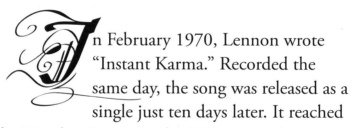

In February 1970, Lennon wrote
"Instant Karma." Recorded the
same day, the song was released as a
single just ten days later. It reached
the Number 3 spot on the U.S. music charts.

Later in the year, Lennon's album, *John
Lennon/Plastic Ono Band,* was released. "I think
it's the best thing I've ever done," Lennon said
about his new solo album. "It's me! And nobody
else. That's why I like it. It's real, that's all."[1]
Lennon felt the music on the new album came
straight from his heart. His childhood feelings

▶ LENNON PERFORMED AT MADISON SQUARE GARDEN IN
NEW YORK IN 1972.

of abandonment and sorrow came through in explosive songs such as "Mother" and "My Mummy's Dead." He had tried to rid himself of these feelings with the help of a psychiatrist. Now he was able to release his painful emotions through his music. Lennon had not lost his touch; the album was highly praised.

September 1971 brought *Imagine*—his best-known solo album. In the title song, Lennon imagined a world free of hunger and conflict, a world where all people could live in peace. "Imagine" is the song most closely associated with the life and dreams of John Lennon.

Ironically, while Lennon was imagining a world filled with peace, he was creating conflict. He and McCartney, once closer than brothers, were now feuding. McCartney had started a new band called Wings, and Lennon thought he heard some insulting remarks about himself on McCartney's new album, *Ram*. Lennon fought back with "How Do You Sleep." This song slammed McCartney's music and jibed that the only good song McCartney had written was "Yesterday." Lennon later said, "If I can't have a fight with my

"'Imagine' was one facet of him. It crystallized his dream for the world, crystallized his idealism. And it was something that he really wanted to say to the world."[2]
—*Yoko Ono*

best friend, I don't know who I can have a fight with."[3] But for a time, the two songwriters were not speaking to each other.

NEW YORK AND THE FBI

On September 3, 1971, shortly after wrapping up work on *Imagine,* Lennon and Ono moved to New York City. As a port city, it reminded him in some ways of Liverpool. And in New York, people left him alone. Lennon's son, Julian, had been only five years old at the time of his parents' divorce and had rarely seen his famous dad after that. Julian was now 11, but with Lennon's move to New York, father and son were an ocean apart.

Although Lennon wanted to settle in the United States, the government did not want him there. The Nixon administration was still mired in the Vietnam War. Lennon was well known as an activist for peace. He wrote the song "Revolution" and had associated with antigovernment activists. But he considered himself a musician first, not a politician. He was not involved in a plot against the government.

However, Lennon was being spied on by the U.S. government. The government's goal was to find a reason to deport him to his home country. In 1972, Nixon ordered the U.S. Immigration and Naturalization Service to begin proceedings to deport Lennon on the basis of a 1968 drug conviction in England. Lennon took the case to court. After years of legal battles, he was granted permanent residency in 1975. Years later, declassified FBI information suggests the U.S. government used the drug conviction because the Beatles, who opposed the Vietnam War, might influence public opinion about the war.

FROM THE "LOST WEEKEND" TO FATHERHOOD

While Lennon was having problems with the FBI, he and Ono were having problems, too. In 1973, Lennon and Ono had moved into a historic apartment building, called the Dakota, overlooking Central Park. But they were not getting along well. Ono felt her career as an artist suffered because she lived in the shadow of Lennon's fame. In October 1973, Ono asked Lennon to move out. They separated for 18 months, a period Lennon called his "Lost Weekend." While away, Lennon had a girlfriend, May Pang, who had been an assistant to Ono and Lennon. Ono not only knew about it, she had suggested he be with Pang, because she knew that Lennon did not like to be alone.

Lennon and Pang went to Los Angeles, where Lennon hooked up with musician friends, including Elton John and Keith Moon of the Who. Lennon's son Julian came for a visit as well. It was one of the few times in Julian's life that he spent with his father. Lennon created music during this period. He recorded the *Walls and Bridges* album that reached Number 1. Elton John played keyboards on Lennon's song "Whatever Gets You Thru the Night," which topped the charts in November 1974.

"Sean was born on October the 9th, which I was, so we're almost like twins. It's a pleasure for me to hang around the house. I was always a homebody. I think a lot of musicians are. I had been so locked in to home environment, and completely switched my way of thinking, that I really didn't think about music at all. My guitar was sort of hung up behind the bed, literally. And I just don't think I took it down in five years."[4]
—*John Lennon*

By early 1975, Lennon returned to Ono, and they soon learned they were expecting a child. On October 9, 1975, on Lennon's thirty-fifth birthday, his son Sean Taro Ono Lennon was born. Lennon had not been around when Julian was a baby. This time, he wanted to be an active father. For a few years, Lennon retired from music and became a "househusband" while Ono handled the couple's business affairs.

In 1980, five years after the birth of Sean, Lennon and Ono began making music together again. Their prior album, *Some Time in New York*

City (1972), had not sold very well. Their new effort, *Double Fantasy*, was their comeback and contained songs by both of them. Lennon's songs included "Beautiful Boy," written for Sean, and "(Just Like) Starting Over." He *was* starting over. At age 40, Lennon believed he had a long career ahead. But tragically, he was wrong.

A LIFE CUT SHORT

In the late afternoon of December 8, 1980, a stranger waited around the Dakota, looking for Lennon. That was not unusual. Fans often stopped at the building, which was well known as the home of the former Beatle. But 25-year-old Mark David Chapman was no ordinary fan—he was mentally ill. He carried a backpack with cassettes of Beatles music, a magazine containing an interview with Lennon, and a .38 handgun.

Chapman had read that Lennon said he did not believe in the Beatles or religion. The comments enraged Chapman. He thought Lennon was a phony. Chapman later claimed that voices in his head urged him to take action. He had come to New York City with one purpose: to kill Lennon.

"I still believe in love and peace. I still believe in positive thinking. . . . I consider that my work won't be finished until I'm dead and buried, and I hope that's a long, long time from now."[5]

—*John Lennon in 1980*

▲ MARK DAVID CHAPMAN

On that December day, at approximately 5:00 p.m., Lennon headed for a limo to go to the recording studio. Chapman stepped forward, holding out the *Double Fantasy* album. Lennon shook Chapman's hand and scrawled out an autograph. A photographer took a photo of Chapman smiling as Lennon signed the album. Chapman had planned to shoot Lennon but was startled by Lennon's kindness. As Lennon's limo sped away, Chapman stayed near the building, waiting into the icy night.

Hours later, at approximately 10:49 p.m., Lennon's car returned. Chapman followed Lennon and Ono as they headed for the entrance before firing five shots into Lennon's back and shoulder. Lennon continued into the entrance of the building before he collapsed in a pool of blood. The police arrived and found Chapman, with his gun, reading a book nearby. Fatally wounded, Lennon was pronounced dead at 11:07 p.m.

Chapman was sentenced to 20 years to life in prison in an upstate New York penitentiary. Chapman has been repeatedly denied parole. Although he has stated that he regrets killing Lennon, it is unclear whether he understands the seriousness of his crime.

Songs Remembering John Lennon

Lennon's legacy lives on through his music. Others have written songs remembering him, including:
- Paul McCartney, "Here Today"
- George Harrison, "All Those Years Ago"
- Elton John, "Empty Garden (Hey Hey Johnny)"
- Queen, "Life Is Real (Song For Lennon)"
- The Kinks, "Killer's Eyes"
- Paul Simon, "The Late Great Johnny Ace"

LENNON'S LEGACY

It did not seem possible that Lennon's clear voice had been silenced. It was a voice that, as part of the most famous band ever, changed rock and roll. His voice had embodied the late sixties. He had spoken out for peace and love and equality at the risk of being ridiculed by the press and targeted by the government. At times, his wisecracking voice was cynical—but it was

▲ The Imagine mosaic that honors Lennon in Central Park

also hopeful. His voice helped define a generation and promised to influence the next. It would live on through his music.

Lennon has not been forgotten. New fans are discovering his music, and his message will live on. A space in Central Park across from the Dakota was named Strawberry Fields in Lennon's honor. A mosaic simply reads, "IMAGINE."

 TIMELINE

1940

John Winston Lennon is born on October 9 in Liverpool, England.

1957

Lennon's mother buys him his first guitar.

1957

Lennon meets McCartney at the Woolton village festival on July 6.

1962

Epstein is hired as manager on January 24.

1962

Best is replaced by Starr in August.

1962

Lennon marries Cynthia Powell August 23. In September, the Beatles record their first single, "Love Me Do."

1958

Lennon's mother is killed on July 15 by a drunk driver.

1960

Lennon forms a group with McCartney, Harrison, and Sutcliffe. Best joins as drummer.

1961

The Beatles debut at the Cavern Club in Liverpool on February 21.

1963

The Beatles record their first album, *Please Please Me*, in February. John Charles Julian Lennon is born April 8.

1963

"I Want to Hold Your Hand" is released in the United States and sells 250,000 copies in three days.

1964

On February 9, the Beatles make their first appearance on the *Ed Sullivan Show*.

IMELINE

1964

In late March, Lennon publishes *In His Own Write*.

1965

Lennon writes the title song for the film *Help!* in January.

1966

The Beatles perform their last live concert August 29 at Candlestick Park. In November, Lennon meets artist Ono.

1969

Lennon and Ono marry on March 20. *Abbey Road* is released September 26.

1970

In April, McCartney announces the Beatles have broken up. *Let It Be* is released May 8.

1970

The album *John Lennon/Plastic Ono Band* is released on December 11.

1967

Lennon writes "I Am the Walrus."

1968

Cynthia Lennon files for divorce on August 22. Lennon and Ono release *Two Virgins* on November 11.

1969

The Beatles' last performance is held January 30 in London.

1971

Lennon and Ono move to New York City. *Imagine* is released on September 9.

1975

Lennon is granted permanent U.S. resident status. Sean Taro Ono Lennon is born on October 9.

1980

Lennon is killed on December 8.

Quick Facts

DATE OF BIRTH
October 9, 1940

PLACE OF BIRTH
Liverpool, England

DATE OF DEATH
December 8, 1980

PLACE OF DEATH
New York City, New York

PARENTS
Alfred Lennon and Julia Stanley Lennon

EDUCATION
Dovedale Primary School, Quarry Bank High School,
Liverpool College of Art

MARRIAGE
Cynthia Powell Lennon (1962–1968)
Yoko Ono (1969–Lennon's death in 1980)

CHILDREN
John Charles Julian Lennon, born April 8, 1963 (with Cynthia
    Powell Lennon)
Sean Taro Ono Lennon, born October 9, 1975 (with Yoko
    Ono Lennon)

IMPORTANT WORKS

Top Albums with the Beatles
Please Please Me (1963)
Meet the Beatles (1964)
A Hard Day's Night (1964)
Help! (1965)
Rubber Soul (1965)
Revolver (1966)
Sgt. Pepper's Lonely Hearts Club Band (1967)
The Beatles (White Album) (1968)
Abbey Road (1969)
Let It Be (1970)

Solo Albums
Imagine (1971)
Walls and Bridges (1974)
Live In New York City (recorded live in 1972) (1986)

Albums with Yoko Ono
Two Virgins (1968)
John Lennon/Plastic Ono Band (1970)
Double Fantasy (1980)

Books
In His Own Write (1964)
A Spaniard in the Works (1965)

QUOTE

"I still believe in love and peace. I still believe in positive thinking. . . . I consider that my work won't be finished until I'm dead and buried, and I hope that's a long, long time from now."—*John Lennon, 1980*

ADDITIONAL RESOURCES

SELECT BIBLIOGRAPHY

The Beatles. *The Beatles Anthology*. San Francisco, CA: Chronicle Books, 2000.

Lennon, Cynthia. *John*. New York, NY: Crown Publishers, 2005.

Norman, Philip. *John Lennon: The Life*. New York, NY: HarperCollins, 2008.

Solt, Andrew and Sam Egan. *Imagine: John Lennon*. New York, NY: Macmillan, 1989.

FURTHER READING

Lennon, John. *In His Own Write*. 1964. New York, NY: Simon and Schuster, 2000.

Lennon, John. *Real Love: The Drawings for Sean*. New York, NY: Random House Children's Books, 1999.

Rappaport, Doreen. *John's Secret Dreams: The Life of John Lennon*. New York, NY: Hyperion Books for Children, 2004.

Turner, Steve. *A Hard Day's Write: The Story Behind Every Beatles Song*. New York, NY: HarperCollins, 1999.

WEB LINKS

To learn more about John Lennon, visit ABDO Publishing Company online at www.abdopublishing.com. Web sites about John Lennon are featured on our Book Links page. These links are routinely monitored and updated to provide the most current information available.

FOR MORE INFORMATION

For more information on this subject, contact or visit the following organizations.

Abbey Road Studios
3 Abbey Road, Saint John's Wood, London NW8 9AY,
United Kingdom
+44 (0) 20 7266 7000
www.abbeyroad.co.uk/visit
The Beatles recorded most of their songs in these studios. It is still a working studio, not a museum, so visitors cannot go inside. However, just outside is the pedestrian crossing where Lennon, McCartney, Harrison, and Starr were famously photographed for their 1969 album *Abbey Road*.

The Beatles Story Visitor Attraction
Britannia Vaults, Albert Dock, Liverpool L3 4AD,
United Kingdom
+44 (0) 151 709 1963
www.beatlesstory.com
This museum is located on the historic Albert Dock in the Beatles' hometown of Liverpool. Visitors can experience the Beatles' story through a series of interactive exhibits. The museum's Web site offers a virtual tour of the highlights.

John Lennon Museum
Saitama Super Arena, 8 Shintoshin, Chuo-ku, Saitama-city,
Saitama 330-9109, Japan
048-601-0009
www.taisei.co.jp/museum/index_e.html
This unique museum contains exhibits from different periods of Lennon's life and showcases memorabilia such as guitars, costumes, and handwritten lyrics.

GLOSSARY

activist
> A person who believes in taking action to bring about political change.

avant-garde
> Art that pushes the boundaries of what is acceptable.

charisma
> A powerful charm or attractiveness.

cheeky
> Boldly impolite.

chord
> A set of three or more different notes played at the same time. Common guitar chords include G, C, and E.

cynical
> Having a negative or critical attitude about human nature.

enigmatic
> Mysterious.

fad
> A fashion that becomes popular for a very short time.

hallucinogenic
> Causing people to see hallucinations, meaning things that are not real.

harmony
> When sounds at different pitches are played or sung at the same time in music and sound pleasant.

idol
>A person or thing that is worshipped or adored.

mania
>Madness or insane passion for something or someone.

melody
>The progression of musical notes that make up a song.

posh
>Elegant and fashionable.

postscript
>An added comment.

psychedelic
>Relating to mind-altering drugs or vivid colors and bizarre patterns.

raucous
>Sounding rough and disorderly.

rendition
>An interpretation or reworking of a song.

riff
>A simple musical element or pattern that is repeated throughout a song.

tempo
>The speed at which a song is played.

SOURCE NOTES

Chapter 1. Beatlemania in America
1. Beatles. *The Beatles Anthology.* San Francisco, CA: Chronicle Books, 2000. 116.
2. Ibid.
3. Beatles press conference, 7 Feb. 1964. *The Beatles Anthology,* Episode 3, Chapter 1. Dir. George Smeaton, Geoff Wonfor. DVD. Los Angeles, CA: Capitol Records, 2002.
4. Clinton Heylin. *Bob Dylan: Behind the Shades Revisited.* New York, NY: W. Morrow, 2001. 148.

Chapter 2. Growing Up in Liverpool
1. Beatles. *The Beatles Anthology.* San Francisco, CA: Chronicle Books, 2000. 7.
2. Philip Norman. *John Lennon: The Life.* New York, NY: HarperCollins, 2008. 34.
3. Beatles. *The Beatles Anthology.* San Francisco, CA: Chronicle Books, 2000. 9.
4. Ibid.
5. Ibid. 10.
6. Ibid. 11.
7. Ibid.

Chapter 3. From Quarry Men to the Beatles
1. Beatles. *The Beatles Anthology.* San Francisco, CA: Chronicle Books, 2000. 20.
2. Ibid. 12.
3. Ibid. 13.
4. Ibid. 14.
5. Andrew Solt and Sam Egan. *Imagine: John Lennon.* New York, NY: Macmillan, 1988. 28.
6. Bob Spitz. *The Beatles: The Biography.* New York, NY: Little, Brown and Co., 2005. 209.
7. Ibid. 293.

8. *The Beatles Anthology*, Episode 1, Chapter 13. Dir. George Smeaton, Geoff Wonfor. DVD. Los Angeles, CA: Capitol Records, 2002.
9. Beatles. *The Beatles Anthology.* San Francisco, CA: Chronicle Books, 2000. 71.
10. Ibid. 70.

Chapter 4. Making It Big
1. Andrew Solt and Sam Egan. *Imagine: John Lennon.* New York, NY: Macmillan, 1988. 60.
2. Beatles. *The Beatles Anthology.* San Francisco, CA: Chronicle Books, 2000. 90.
3. Ibid.
4. Ibid.
5. Andrew Solt and Sam Egan. *Imagine: John Lennon.* New York, NY: Macmillan, 1988. 48.
6. Gould, Jonathan. *Can't Buy Me Love: The Beatles, Britain, and America.* New York, NY: Harmony Books, 2007. 168.
7. Beatles. *The Beatles Anthology.* San Francisco, CA: Chronicle Books, 2000. 102.

Chapter 5. International Fame
1. Andrew Solt and Sam Egan. *Imagine: John Lennon.* New York, NY: Macmillan, 1988. 63.
2. Bob Spitz. *The Beatles: The Biography.* New York, NY: Little, Brown and Co., 2005. 501.
3. Beatles. *The Beatles Anthology.* San Francisco, CA: Chronicle Books, 2000. 134.
4. Ibid. 187.
5. Bob Spitz. *The Beatles: The Biography.* New York, NY: Little, Brown and Co., 2005. 582.
6. Andrew Solt and Sam Egan. *Imagine: John Lennon.* New York, NY: Macmillan, 1988. 106.

SOURCE NOTES
CONTINUED

7. Bob Spitz. *The Beatles: The Biography*. New York, NY: Little, Brown and Co., 2005. 181.
8. Ibid. 180.

Chapter 6. Controversy and Change
1. Bob Spitz. *The Beatles: The Biography*. New York, NY: Little, Brown and Co., 2005. 627.
2. Ibid. 632–633.
3. Larry Kane. *Lennon Revealed*. Philadelphia, PA: Running Press, 2005. 56.
4. Cynthia Lennon. *John*. New York, NY: Crown Publishers, 2005. 169.
5. David Sheff. Interview with John Lennon, September 8–28, 1980. *Playboy*. Jan. 1981. 22 July 2009 <http://www.john-lennon.com/playboyinterviewwithjohnlennonandyokoono.htm>.

Chapter 7. The Psychedelic Years
1. Beatles. *The Beatles Anthology*. San Francisco, CA: Chronicle Books, 2000. 236.
2. Ibid. 242.
3. Jann S. Wenner and Joe Levy, eds. Interview with John Lennon, 21 Jan. 1971. *The Rolling Stone Interviews*. New York, NY: Back Bay Books, 2007. 39.
4. Ibid. 45.
5. Beatles. *The Beatles Anthology*. San Francisco, CA: Chronicle Books, 2000. 273.
6. Ibid. 301.

Chapter 8. Love, Peace, and an End to the Beatles

1. Bob Spitz. *Yeah! Yeah! Yeah! The Beatles, Beatlemania, and the Music That Changed the World*. New York, NY: Little, Brown and Co., 2007. 207.
2. David Sheff. Interview with John Lennon, September 8–28, 1980. *Playboy*. Jan. 1981. 22 July 2009 <http://www.john-lennon.com/playboyinterviewwithjohnlennonandyokoono.htm>.
3. Bob Spitz. *The Beatles: The Biography*. New York, NY: Little, Brown and Co., 2005. 804.
4. Ibid. 805.
5. Beatles. *The Beatles Anthology*. San Francisco, CA: Chronicle Books, 2000. 302.
6. Philip Norman. *John Lennon: The Life*. New York, NY: HarperCollins, 2008. 606.
7. David Sheff. Interview with John Lennon, September 8–28, 1980. *Playboy*. Jan. 1981. 22 July 2009 <http://www.john-lennon.com/playboyinterviewwithjohnlennonandyokoono.htm>.

Chapter 9. America, Fatherhood, and Tragedy

1. Jann S. Wenner and Joe Levy, eds. "Interview with John Lennon," pub. 21 Jan. 1971. *The Rolling Stone Interviews*. New York, NY: Back Bay Books, 2007. 33.
2. Yoko Ono. *Imagine: John Lennon*. Dir. Andrew Solt. DVD. Burbank, CA: Warner Home Video, 2005.
3. John Lennon and Yoko Ono on *The Mike Douglas Show*. 18 Feb. 1972. *Mike Douglas Show with John Lennon & Yoko Ono*. VHS. Rhino/Wea, 1998.
4. John Lennon. *Imagine: John Lennon*. Dir. Andrew Solt. DVD. Burbank, CA: Warner Home Video, 2005.
5. Ibid.

INDEX

 About the Author

Jennifer Joline Anderson has been writing since she was a teenager. She won a contest and had her first short story published in *Seventeen* magazine. Today she lives in St. Paul, Minnesota, where she writes and edits books for young people.

 Photo Credits

Robert Whitaker/Getty Images, cover, 3; Land of Lost Content/Photolibrary, 7, 55, 59, 97 (top); AP Images, 11, 15, 25, 53, 57, 59, 67, 72, 75, 77, 79, 82, 87, 92, 97 (bottom), 98 (top), 98 (bottom), 99; The Print Collector/Photolibrary, 17; Rex Butcher/Photolibrary, 20; Redferns/Getty Images, 22; STR/AP Images, 27, 96; Astrid Kirchherr/Redferns/Getty Images, 33; Jewish Chronical/Photolibrary, 37; David Farrell/ Getty Images, 39; Photolibrary, 44; Central Press/Stringer/ Getty Images, 47; Max Scheler/Redferns/Getty Images, 49; Bob Thomas/Getty Images, 65; Capitol Records/Photofest, 69; Fabian Bimmer/AP Images, 85; Ellen Rooney/Photolibrary, 95